YOUR KNOWLEDGE HAS VALUE

Bibliographic information published by the German National Library:

The German National Library lists this publication in the National Bibliography; detailed bibliographic data are available on the Internet at http://dnb.dnb.de .

Imprint:

Copyright © 2015 GRIN Verlag, Open Publishing GmbH
Print and binding: Books on Demand GmbH, Norderstedt Germany
ISBN: 978-3-668-06281-8

This book at GRIN:

http://www.grin.com/en/e-book/308067/hopes-and-dreams-of-black-us-citizens-as-portrayed-in-lorraine-hansberry-s

Annika Fußbroich

Hopes and dreams of black US citizens as portrayed in Lorraine Hansberry's "A Raisin in the Sun"

GRIN Publishing

GRIN - Your knowledge has value

Since its foundation in 1998, GRIN has specialized in publishing academic texts by students, college teachers and other academics as e-book and printed book. The website www.grin.com is an ideal platform for presenting term papers, final papers, scientific essays, dissertations and specialist books.

Visit us on the internet:

http://www.grin.com/

http://www.facebook.com/grincom

http://www.twitter.com/grin_com

März 2015

What happens to a dream deferred?
opes and fears of black US citizens as portrayed in Lorraine Hansberry's "A Raisin in the Sun"

Annika Fußbroich

Stufe 11

Schuljahr 2014/2015

Content

1. Choice of topic

During my time in the US as a foreign exchange student, I learned a lot about the American Dream and the American way of living. Since I have always been interested in the history and traditions of this country, I had certain knowledge about America's racial problems today and in the past as well as its firm belief that every individual has the power to attain self-fulfillment and achieve any aim - before ever learning about it in class.

But on account of talking about the US in school, I realized that I had never giving much thought to those who have to face greater obstacles to make their dreams come true. In this particular case, I was thinking about black US citizens, a group of people which always seemed to have special problems – and even today, they are still not treated as equal members of society. Consequently, I was wondering if their dreams differ from those of the white population somehow. What do they fear? What are their greatest hopes and dreams? And is there even a difference between those "types" American Dreams?

As a result, my research paper will take a closer look on Lorraine Hansberry's "A Raisin in the Sun" and the therein portrayed Younger family, a financially suffering black family living in Chicago in the 1950s.

This play seemed to be a great basis for research and analysis to me because it was written by a black woman who experienced discrimination herself. As a result, Lorraine Hansberry had dreams deferred, too, so that is why her work manifests itself as very vivid and credible.

2. Plot overview

The play *"A raisin in the Sun"*, written between 1953 and 1956 by Lorraine Hansberry, portrays a few significant weeks in the life of the Youngers, a black and financially suffering family living in Chicago's Southside during the 1950.

The Younger family consists of five members: Mama, Walter Lee, Ruth, Beneatha, and Travis. Mama's husband is recently deceased, so she is now living together in an undersized apartment as the head of the family together with her two children, Walter Lee and Beneatha. Walter Lee is married to Ruth and they have a son together, Travis.

The entire play takes place in the Younger's living room. When it opens, the family is impatiently waiting for a $10,000 check from Mr. Younger's life insurance.

However, there is disagreement as to use this considerable sum: Mama dreams of buying a little house to escape the uncomfortable apartment and to provide more space for the family and so does Ruth. Walter Lee would rather invest the money in a liquor store he would run with his friends, and Beneatha needs some of the value to pay for her medial school tuition.

As the action of the play progresses, we see that the different aims of the adult family members collide, which is the trigger for a lot of disputes and tension among them:

Mama makes a down payment of $3,500 on a house in Clybourne Park, a white neighborhood. This decision incurs both of her children's anger: Beneatha is, because her Nigerian boyfriend Joseph Asagai set her thinking, trying to find her roots and her cultural identity in Africa, and as a consequence, she blames her mother for trying to assimilate to the white society by buying a house in a white neighborhood.

Walter, who alleges himself for not earning enough money to provide his family an appropriate standard of living, dreams of being self-employed and financially stable. Running an own liquor store is the key to wealth in his opinion. Thus, it is incomprehensible for him that his mother will not invest the money from the life insurance in their future but in a house. Her undertake enrages her son incredibly, yet he has to give in to his mother because she is rightful owner of the money.

A few weeks later, Mama finally decides to entrust his son with the remaining $6,500 under the condition that he has to deposit some of it into a bank account with the intention to safe it for

4

Beneatha's college tuition. Although it is incommensurate with her idea of a good Christian to run a liquor store, she decides due to her love for her son to take this step which seemed to satisfy all persons involved.

The Younger's are now all very enthusiastic about the moving when Karl Lindner, a representative of the Clybourne Park Improvement Association, pays them a visit. He carefully explains that the colored family is unwanted in the white neighborhood and that the community raised money to buy off the Younger's house. The Youngers, however, are furious about this offer and refuse it.

The same day, Bobo, an affiliate of Walter, enters and brings dreadful news: Willy Harris, the man that ought to take care of the money invested in the liquor store, disappeared with the entire sum, including the amount that was meant for Beneatha's college tuition.

Despite the hopeless situation, the Younger's move out of their apartment into the new house with the determination to master their problems as a family and to have no longer dreams deferred.

3. Characterization of the main characters with special emphasis on their hopes and dreams

3.1 Lena Younger:

Lena Younger, for the most part called "Mama", is the head of the Younger family after her husband Walter passed away only recently. In the stage directions, she is described as a "woman in her early sixties, full bodies and strong"[1]. Mama has grey hair, a dark-brown skin and her face is marked by all the hardship she had to endure all her life, yet she kept a certain kind of beauty and dignity over the years. Moreover, her carriage gets something out of her African roots. [2]

Mama is a very loving and caring person; helpfulness and the urge to share in her family's joy and sorrow are consequently a basic part of her nature. In addition to that, devoutness and

---

[1] Hansberry page 69
[2] See Ebd. page 70

Christian ideals are the two things with whom she accounts her decisions and her behavior:[3] this character trait of hers is vividly illustrated when Mama refuses to entrust Walter Lee the money from the life insurance, not because she thinks he is poor businessman, but due to her attitude to morality that running a liquor store is flagrant. [4] This rather conservative view causes conflicts with her two children, but especially with Beneatha who sees herself as an emancipated young woman who does not need God in her life.[5]

Despite the Younger's constantly unstable financial conditions, it had always been Lena's and Big Walter's dream to own a house. Ironically, this dream could only come true with the help of Big Walter's life insurance which is eventually affiliated with his death. As a result, Lena is very eager to use the money as he would have wished it, so when she finds out that her son let it go to waste, she is very furious and fierce.[6] [7]

In addition to that, proof can be found that Lena is either an incurable optimist or just blind for the dangers possibly waiting for her family: she was for example warned by her neighbor Mrs. Johnsons that blacks were often violated in white vicinities[8], moreover, she completely ignored the doubts uttered by her children concerning Clybourne Park. But again, this shows that her desire to leave her current behind neighborhood behind is extremely distinctive.

3.2 Walter Younger:

Walter Younger, Ruth's husband and Beneatha's brother, is an approximately 30 year old man living with his family in Chicago's Southside. He works for a white upper class family as a chauffeur, a job that makes him feel very unsatisfied as it is an expression for the superiority of whites over blacks in his opinion. Walter Lee tends to behave passionate, but also volatile[9], which is the reason for him to believe that "nobody in this house is ever going to understand [him]."[10]

As a consequence, Walter usually blames impudently other people, women in particular, for his failure in life - he has a chauvinistic, old-fashioned portrayal of women in general.

Despite Walter's lack of education and his color of skin, he has the ambitious dream to run his

---

[3] See Ulm page 22f
[4] See Hansberry page 109
[5] See Ebd. page 85
[6] See Ebd. page 184
[7] Ulm page 23
[8] See Hanaberry page 150
[9] Ebd. page 25
[10] See Hansberry page 69

own liquor store with whom he wants to provide luxury and affluence for his family.[11] By the choice of his work environment, we can conclude that Christian values and traditions are not as significant for him as they are for his mother and to finance this enormous enterprise, Walter Lee would like to make use of the money from his father's life insurance for which Big Walter had to work very hard.[12] Thus, his mother denies this request, so that Walter Lee feels hurt and again very misunderstood.[13] On account of his poor scholastic education, Walter is not capable to run an own business or to make wise economic decisions, so consequently, he loses all the entrusted money to the criminal Willy Harris. Yet, it is money that is most desirable thing for him, by a long way more important than personal qualities in his opinion. Walter Lee's dreams consist of material prosperity, so when he tells his son about his business idea, he goes into raptures about mansions and servants.[14] Moreover, he has only very little cultural and historic knowledge, which can be seen by his conviction that Prometheus is only neologism invented by George Murchison to boast.

To put in a nutshell, one can say that Walter main problem is his inability to see the difference between reality and his ambitious dreams. By holding on to the idea he could run a liquor store so desperately, he does not only bring misfortune on himself, but on the entire family. Walter Lee becomes aware of his responsibility towards the people he loves for the first time when he shows the moral strength to reject Lindner's offer- this turns him in a duty-bound father, son and husband.[15]

3.3 Beneatha Younger:

Beneatha Younger is the daughter of Lena and Big Walter, about 20 year old and still living with her family in Chicago's Southside. She and her brother do not only look very similar, but they furthermore share values towards life and success. Ruth herself says: "I guess I always think things have more emphasis if they are big, somehow."[16]. Consequently, Beneatha has the ambition to start an academic career as a doctor as the only person in her family who would have necessary qualities to do so. Apart from that, she is the embodiment of an emancipated, gifted and independent woman who can only find self-realization in a profession she loves- to

---

[11] See Hansberry page 25
[12] See Hansberry page 184
[13] See Ebd. page 109
[14] See Hansberry page 159
[15] See Hansberry page 26f
[16] Hansberry page 161

7

be exactly, this is the dream she is trying to achieve desperately. Unfortunately, she has to face many obstacles: her brother, who has a very conservative image of women, thinks she would rather work as a nurse because of her gender[17], and no doubt, her color of skin will not make it any easier for her to be successful. Above all, the medical school is going to cost a considerably amount of money the family does not have[18]- but apart from all those difficulties, Beneatha will not give up on her dreams.

Yet, she shows some character traits that are not very appealing: although her family is obviously financially suffering[19], she allows herself expensive hobbies like guitar lessons. It seems that Beneatha has a right to enjoy these privileges due to her outstanding education. Owing to her boyfriend Joseph Asagai, she shows great interest in her African roots and departs more and more from the American way of living: thus, George Murchison's efforts to assimilate into the white society are incomprehensible and disgraceful in her opinion. [20]

4. Lorraine Hansberry's biography and political engagement and its impact on the play

Lorraine Vivien Hansberry was born on May 19, 1930 as the youngest child of a wealthy middleclass family living in Chicago. Although her parents would have been able to provide an agreeable vicinity, her family lived in Chicago's Southside due to racial segregation just like the protagonists of her play *A Raisin in the Sun*. On account of living in a district full of poverty and desperation, the author witnessed many destitute families' living conditions and their lack of everyday needs. But instead of trying to stand out from the less fortunate children in her neighborhood, she was fascinated by them and attempted to gain their friendship.[21] Hansberry herself said that "from this moment I became – a rebel."[22]

But when she was 7 years old, the family moved into an exclusively white neighborhood. The new neighbors felt endangered by the Blacks, so there were physical, but also psychological penetrations. Hansberry herself said, that "[her] memories [...] include being spat at, cursed

---

[17] See Hansberry page 66
[18] See Hansberry page 66
[19] See Ebd. page 54
[20] See Ebd. page 145
[21] See Ulm page 3f
[22] See Nemiroff page 51

and pummeled in the daily trek to and from school."[23]

And again, there is common ground between Lorraine Hansberry's biography and the play she wrote: both families, the Youngers and the Hansberrys, were very unwelcome in their neighborhood and the reason to reconsider moving would have been in both cases not the lack of money, but white racism.[24]

After graduating from high school, the author moved to Harlem, New York, the center of Afro-American culture those days.[25] To provide a living, she worked as a waitress and cashier, but apart from those rather modest employments, she attended Jefferson School for Social Sciences[26] and became politically active in conjunction with Paul Robeson and W.E.B. DuBois whose principal objectives were the introduction of absolute equality for colored citizens and the abolition of racial dividing lines. Hansberry showed next to that special interest in the emancipation of women. In 1953, she married Robert Nemiroff, a white Jewish writer with Russian roots, who is besides that, a political activist.[27] Certainly, the man of her choice reflects her anti-racist and open-minded worldview.

Between 1953 and 1956, Lorraine Hansberry started to work on play that would soon be known as *A Raisin in the Sun*. It opened on March 11, 1959 on Broadway as the first play to be written by a black female playwright and also won the New York Drama Critics' Circle's "Best Play of the Year" Award. Despite all the attention the play compelled to due awarding, it is its content that went down to history: *"A Raisin in the Sun* […] was not only the portrayal of contemporary black life, but also […] predicted the exploration, explosion and assertion of black identity, heritage and beauty; the inevitable linking of the civil rights movement in American with the anti-colonialist struggles in Africa; second-wave feminism: and the ultimate connection of all of these issues to human freedom."[28]

During the 1960s, Hansberry worked on several other plays, for example *Les Blancs* or *The Drinking Gourd*,[29] even though she was diagnosed cancer in May 1963. Moreover, she supported the protest against the oppression of blacks vigorously and participated in rallies and discussions herself. However, she was not able to be a part of Martin Luther King's famous "I

---

[23] Ebd. page 51
[24] See Ulm page 47
[25] See Ebd. page 6
[26] Hansberry page 38f
[27] See Ulm page 6f
[28] See Hansberry page 40
[29] See Ebd. page 40

have a Dream" speech, yet she predicted that this day would go down in American history. In March 1964, her marriage with Robert Nemiroff was dissolved; nevertheless, they still had a rapport to each other.

Lorraine Hansberry died on January 12, 1965 at the age of only 34 and was buried in Croton-on-Hudson, where she had lived the years preceding her death.

In addition to that, a commemorative service was held in Harlem among whose participants were Paul Robeson and Langston Hughes.[30]

So in conclusion, it is clear that *A Raisin in the Sun* was decisively influenced by the author's personal experiences and ideas: the Hansberrys' living situation was very similar to the one the Youngers had to endure, and they both try to find their way out of it by moving into a white neighborhood. Furthermore, Beneatha Younger shows many character traits comparable to Lorraine Hansberry's, the two women tried equally to receive for example an outstanding education, but also to be emancipated and independent. In addition to that, Hansberry expressed her firm belief that assimilating into the white society equals self-denial by creating a character like George Murchison, a black man who is completely integrated into the white upper class. As a consequence, he is very much disliked by the Youngers[31]- they just cannot identify with his way of living, and so could not Lorraine Hansberry. By portraying them as a family who is eager to improve their life, the author made a clear statement concerning black inferiority: the Youngers are not willing to behave like they were white, yet, they want a peaceful and dignified life alongside those who try to oppress them. They are willing to beat the odds, but they will not fight for their rights violently- an idea also mirrored by Martin Luther King in his "I have a Dream" speech.

The black American Dream- a dream deferred?

The American Dream is a myth that developed over the centuries, but the term itself was first introduced by James Truslow Adams in 1931 in order to describe what made America so attractive for millions of immigrants from all over the world, but "surprisingly, there is no

---

[30] See Ulm page 7f
[31] See Ulm page 51

consensus in terms of a fixed definition about it[32], however, the following description can be found in A. Rosenbaum's *"The Penguin Encyclopedia of American History"*:

33   *"a nebulous term, much abused by politicians, that seems to have evolved from the early immigrants' and pioneers' hopes for lives of political and religious and personal independence in the New World to a largely materialistic expectation of upward social mobility and ever-increaasing affluence"*

The first people coming to America were European settlers that tried to escape religious persecution, political oppression and poverty in their homelands. So consequently, they hoped for a better life in the new world by achieving prosperity, freedom, a classless society with equal opportunities, democracy, just as well as, happiness, dignity and religious freedom. On account of the influx of people from all kinds of nations and the strong upholding of beliefs and values associated with the American Dream, the US became prospering and growing multicultural and ethnical diverse nation – with good cause, 8 out of the 10 richest people in the world are US citizens[34]. Furthermore, America always liked to see itself as an open-minded country that happily welcomes all kinds of people who want to become a part of the huge "melting pot" (cf. the Latin motto "e pluribus unum"). Yet this dream never came true due to refusal of many immigrants to assimilate into the American society by giving up their national identity, as well as their culture and language. Especially in the 1960s, the growing self-confidence of ethnic minorities and the influx of immigrants that do not want to be absorbed by the American society caused a reconsideration of the "melting pot" idea- nowadays, the term "salad bowl" is suggested to illustrate that people of all ethnic backgrounds will life jointly together, yet they are not absorbing one another. [35]

But how does the black American Dream differ from the one other groups of immigrants had when they were looking for self-fulfillment far away from home? **It does not.** Blacks and whites do share the exact same dreams, the only thing that is completely different are the obstacles they had to face (and still have to) in order to make their dreams come true.

36   " For much of American history, male-dominated society in the US has forced women, Native Americans, African Americans, Asian Americans and Latinos into inferior categories."

[32] Klopsch page 4
[33] Rosenbaum page 12
[34] Focus Money Online: *Das sind die reichsten Menschen der Welt.* 03.03.2014, 15:57
[35] Sicher ins Abitur, Ernst Klett Verlag GmbH, Stuttgart 2006
[36] Mauk/ Oakland page 68

Like many other writers, Lorraine Hansberry expounds the American Dream in her works and critically asks, what basic values for the society in general, but also for the black minority in particular mean. Therefore, she states the inhuman living conditions of many colored citizens those days and stresses their legitimate demands on freedom, equality and self-fulfillment. It was Hansberry's firm belief that the American Dream will come true for Afro-Americans, too.[37] Thus, she created characters that reflect her optimistic world view. To underline to underline this statement, I will examine the dreams of the protagonists of *A Raisin in the Sun*.

Lena Younger has always dreamed, together with her husband, of owning an own house. Sadly, this dream could only come true because of Mr. Younger's death, as she has now the money from his life insurance at her disposal. Since their mutual dream did not die together with him, one of the Lena's first undertakings once the check arrived in the mail is to make a down payment on a house in a decent neighborhood. Her behavior shows that house ownership is, just like for all the people in her new neighborhood, a most basic want for whom she exerts herself. Actually you can call house ownership a part of the American Dream[38] Yet, there is a considerable difference between her and her without exception white neighbors: she had to wait all her life long in order to make this wish come true, most of them take their elevated living situation for granted. In order to contrast the inappropriate living conditions of the Youngers with those of people living in nicer accommodations, she puts great emphasis on describing the disadvantages of inhabiting an apartment in Chicago's Southside.[39] The apartment is even called a "rat trap"[40] by the Youngers.[41]

So consequently, the description of their future house is much more optimistic:
[42]

> „ Three bedrooms – nice big one for you and Ruth...me and Beneatha still have to share our room, but Travis have one of his own [...] and there's a yard with a little patch of dirt where I could maybe get to grow me a few flowers [...] I don't want to make it sound fancier that it is...It's just a plain little old house – but it's made good and solid – and it will be ours. Walter Lee- it makes a difference in a man when he can walk on floors that belong to him."

---

[37] See Ulm page 44
[38] See Klopsch page 14
[39] See Tindal / Shi page 1105
[40] See Hansberry page 77
[41] See Klopsch page 19
[42] Hansberry page 138

Mama is not the only one in the family who has great dreams: Walter Lee, her son, dreams of being a rich and successful businessman. Thus, material prosperity and upward mobility are parts of his self-fulfillment, just like they are for many other white Americans. Walter Lee focuses on money when he speaks about the pursuit of personal happiness. He even insists that "[money] is life"[43]. This remark is absolutely shocking for his mother[44] who tries to attain self-fulfillment by pursing intangible dreams, other than for her son, for whom money is the key to satisfaction.

Thus, his family's lack of financial means makes him feel ashamed and angry, not just because he cannot offer them a sophisticated standard of living, but due to his fear to be seen as a failure. The Dream of Upward Mobility is a "desire to achieve beyond one's parents' economic status or ensure a child's greater success in life"[45], so Walter Lee's American Dream is basically connected to his hopes to change his social status by moving upwards on the "ladder of success"[46]. On this behalf, it is very interesting that he does not directly blame the color of his skin for his unattainable dreams, but just himself. Yet, Walter Lee is very eager to change the current situation by running a liquor store successfully. Other than his sister, he does not want to carry out this enterprise by "transformation through education"[47], but sees his only chance in the money from the life insurance. Walter Lee does not only want acquire standing, he also wants to be prosperous. The extent of the over-estimation of his abilities become clear to the reader when he goes into raptures about the tangible goods the family will own one day.

for Ruth – maybe a Cadillac convertible to do her shopping in."
[48]

"And I'll pull up the car up on the driveway…just a plain black Chrysler, I think with white walls - no – black tyres. More elegant. Rich people don't have to be flashy…though I'll have to get something a little sportier for Ruth – maybe a Cadillac convertible to do her shopping in."

This quotation helps the reader to better understand his pompous dreams- he does not only want to be member middle class without financial worries, but he wants a life with excessive

---

[43] Hansberry page 113
[44] See ebd.
[45] Sawhill /Morton page 7
[46] Ernst Klett Verlag
[47] Cullen page 60
[48] Hansberry page 159

luxury.

And although his aims in life seem to be unrealistic, it is not said that they are extraordinary: there are many Americans of all ethnic backgrounds that want to move up the ladder of success and to be businesspeople. There are for example a lot of Native American tribes that became successful in business due to their discovery that they can create popular attractions on their land[50] - so as far as the question goes if Walter Lee's business idea is too unorthodox, one can name that there have already been more unconventional enterprises.

The last person in the family with outstanding ambitious is Beneatha. It is her greatest dream to become a doctor – and it seems like she is able to overcome all the odds in her way. Her biggest problem is her lack of financial means to pay for her medical tuition. Every so often, she is reminded, especially by her brother, that her studies consume an enormous amount of money. Instead of supporting his sister, he is trying to make her feel guilty.

[51]

> „Who the hell told you you had to be a doctor? If you're so crazy 'bout messing 'round with sick people – then be a nurse like other woman – or just get married and be quiet...

This statement underlines in addition to that the attitude of most people in that time towards independent and emancipated women. They were the target of peoples' ridicule and were not judges by their abilities and skills, but by their gender. Women that live the dream of upward mobility and the pursuit of their own happiness did hardly exist in the 1950s, and therefore, it is even more remarkable that Beneatha as a member of the black society is so eager to prove the society wrong. Moreover, the profession of her choice is extraordinary, too: she wants to study medicine, which is a very fastidious and demanding major. Just like for her brother, she knows that the color of her skin causes rather difficult living conditions, and that they are caught in vicious circle of poor education and poverty. Yet, they are the ones who are more than willing to leave those negatives things behind and start a color-blind career according to the idea of Morton and Sawhill who compiled the thesis that upward mobility means to achieve beyond your parents' social status[52]. And Beneatha is definitely interested in moving up the ladder of success, and "transformation through education"[53] is for her the key to prosperity.

---

[50] Green Line 4 page 55
[51] Hansberry page 68
[52] Sawhill/Morton page 7
[53] Cullen page 60

Another important aspect of the American Dream as we know it from white Americans is the belief in individualism. Beneatha does not want to rely on anyone else than herself, and she sees it as her own responsibility to be successful in life, just according to the saying "every man is the architect of his own future".

So after having analyzed the hopes and the dreams of the protagonists, there is no doubt that they have to overcome many obstacles, a lot more than a white family would have, in order to achieve their objectives.

Certainly, one can assume that due to the fact there is an open ending to the play, none of the characters presented will ever reach their life aims. But that does not mean that the black American Dream is a dream deferred, it is just a dream that is constantly obstructed. But as a matter of fact, there are always ways to make your aims come true: for the Younger, the money from the life insurance was the actual key to a life they always dreamed of. Losing it was an incredible retrograde step, however, because of the fact that the money was in the receipt of the Younger's for a short while, we see that even the most unfortunate ones will have a little luck in life once. Furthermore, the Younger never actually gave up chasing their dreams: Mama lived in the tiny apartment for decades, yet she never stopped dreaming of a better accommodation – her spirit has not extinguished just because it took so long!

Another great example for this unbreakable attitude can be found when Walter turns down the money from Mr. Lindner's offer[54]: although the situation is worse than ever and the family is in desperate need of the money, they decide mutually that accepting the fresh offer from the Clybourne Park Improvement Association would equal libel of their pride and their dreams. However, it needs to be said that the Younger's stand for all people who are unable to make their individual outline of life come true. And those people are black in particular since they have to defer their dreams more often than others. However, we always need to keep in ind that a dream deferred is not a dream that does no longer exist. The disastrous living conditions deprive the Youngers of their future prospects, so it is even more remarkable that they are still hoping and fighting.

---

[54] Hanberry page 208

The common ground between Langston Hughes "*Harlem*" and Lorraine Hansberry's "*A Raisin in the Sun*"

Harlem[55]

What happens to a dream deferred?

Does it dry up

like a raisin in the sun?

Or fester like a sore—

And then run?

Does it stink like rotten meat?

Or crust and sugar over—

like a syrupy sweet?

Maybe it just sags

like a heavy load.

Or does it explode?

- LANGSTON HUGHES

The available poem *"Harlem"* was published in 1951 by the Afro-American writer Langston Hughes. As it can be seen easily, the third line of this poem was eponymous for Lorraine Hansberry's play *"A Raisin in the Sun"*. Both works deal with the problems of the black American population and the unattainability of their dreams.

---

[55] Hansberry page 45

When *"Harlem"* was published in 1951, the embitterment of Afro-American US citizens reached its peak and was in search of an outlet. Almost one century after the Abolition of Slavery in the United States, the black were still in inferior group of citizens and deprived in most parts of the public life. Many of those discriminated were very eager to change their current situation, but of course, this major transformation cannot happen from one day to next. Likewise, there was no guarantee that any of the revolutionary endeavors will be rewarded with a successful outcome. And so the thought of what will happen if all the attempts to improve the life of black citizens will remain futile struck in the peoples' heads.

The first line "What happens to a dream deferred?" of the poem *"Harlem"* is based on this tense historical background. As an answer to the question, the author uses many metaphors from the everyday life in the first part of the poem to illustrate the feeling of frustration and perplexity: maybe the dream dries up like a raisin in the sun, but maybe it will be sugarcoated like sticky sweet. What all of his named comparisons have in common is their very negative connotation, just like the fact that all the disgusting things happening to the referred examples ensue because of peoples' inaction.

In the second part of the poem, which is rather short compared to the first part, the Langston Hughes offers another possibility of what could happen to this dream deferred: it could just sink into the subconscious of the affected person and stay there as an omnipresent burden. This comparison reminds the reader of Sigmund Freud's psychoanalytical dream theory, where it is said that a dream suppressed will eventually cause permanent psychic illness.

In the last line, written in italic letters, the most disastrous possible consequence is mentioned: what happens if all the pent-up anger suddenly unloads?[56]

By taking up the core issue of the poem *"Harlem"*, Lorraine Hansberry alludes once again to the problematical situation of Afro-Americans, but she furthermore stresses that she is not the only making efforts to point out problematic nature that is omnipresent, but most extensively ignored by most parts of the society.

What *A Raisin in the Sun* and *Harlem* have in common is their focus on the effect of racism. They both do not portray certain incidents of it in particular, but they show its consequences in daily life as well as its psychological effects on the affected persons.

In *"A Raisin in the Sun"*, the Younger's suffer from very bad living conditions caused by the

---

[56] Ulm page 45f

racist attitude of the society. In the poem *"Harlem"*, the consequences of pent-up frustration and anger are described. They both deal with important choices with unknown outcome that are weighted against broken dream that might never ever become really.

Furthermore, there is very interesting connection between the two writers: Hansberry seemed to be inspired by Hughes' works; she even took the poem *"Harlem"* as the epigraph of her play *"A Raisin in the Sun"*, and the central question, *What happens to a dream deferred?*, is similar, too.

After all, both works have a significant impact on literature and society nowadays, as well as in the time when they were written. They criticize and warn the society that the bad treatment of the black society will eventually lead to a catastrophe, and that it is impossible hold back hopes forever.

Bibliography

Literature:

Hansberry, Lorraine: *A Raisin in the Sun*. Reclam. Stuttgart 2012

Secondary literature:

Cullen, Jim. *The American Dream – A Short History of an Idea that Shaped a Nation*. Oxford: Oxford University Press, 2003.

Ernst Klett Verlag: *Green Line 4 für Klasse 8 an Gymnasien*. Stuttgart 2012

Klopsch, Nadja: *The American Dream in the 20th Century*. Bachlor Thesis. Ernst-Moritz-Arndt-Universität Greifswald

Mauk, David/ Oakland, John: *American Civilization. An Introduction*. New York: Routledge, 2004.

Nemiroff, Robert (Hrsg.): *To Be Young, Gifted and Black*. Signet, New American Library, Penguin (USA): New York 1970

Rosenbaum, Robert A., ed. *The Penguin Encyclopedia of American History*. New York: Viking Adult, 2003.

Tidall, George Brown/ Shi, David Emory: *America: A Narrative History*. New York: W.W. Norton & Company, 2000.

Ulm, Dieter: *Interpretation Englisch: A Raisin in the Sun*. Stark. o.O. 2012

Online sources:

o.A.: *Das sind die reichsten Menschen der Welt*. Focus Money Online. 03.03.2014, 15:57: http://www.focus.de/finanzen/news/76-milliarden-us-dollar-schwer-bill-gates-ist-wieder-der-reichste-mensch-der-welt_id_3657779.html

Sawhill, Isabell/ Morton, John E.: *"Economic Mobility. Is the American Dream Alive and Well?"*, 20.Oktober2008:<http://www.economicmobility.org/assets/pdfs/EMP_American_Dream.pdf>

YOUR KNOWLEDGE HAS VALUE